The Right to Vote

By Teri Crawford Jones

MODERN CURRICULUM PRESS
Pearson Learning Group

The following people from Pearson Learning Group have contributed to the development of this product:

Art and Design: Salita Mehta, Elizabeth Nemeth, Alison O'Brien

Editorial: Leslie Feierstone Barna, Nicole Iorio, Jennie Rakos, Jennifer Serra

Inventory: Levon Carter

Marketing: Alison Bruno

Production: Roxanne Knoll

Photographs: Cover: The Granger Collection, New York. 4: David Friedman/Getty Images, Inc. 6: Bob Daemmrich/Stock Boston. 9, 11: © North Wind Picture Archives. 12–13: © Bettmann/Corbis. 14–15: © AP/Wide World Photo. 16–17: *bkgd* © Bettmann/Corbis. 16: *inset l.*, inset *r.* Courtesy of the Library of Congress. 18–19: © Bettmann/Corbis. 20–21: © Bob Daemmrich/PhotoEdit.

ISBN-13: 978-1-4284-0874-6

ISBN-10: 1-4284-0874-6

Printed in the United States of America
1 2 3 4 5 6 7 8 9 10 11 10 09 08 07

Modern Curriculum Press
Pearson Learning Group

1-800-321-3106
www.pearsonlearning.com

Contents

People vote in elections to decide who will be our country's leaders.

Who Chooses in Our Country?

On one fall night, your phone keeps ringing. People call to tell the adults in your family to vote. On Election Day, U.S. citizens vote for who should lead the nation.

Americans today may wonder if their votes matter. Citizens may not feel that they are part of the national government. Yet, the government in our country works well because of the people. The people of our country choose government officials. In some countries, people cannot share their **views** or vote for leaders. Even in our country, all people did not always have the **freedom** to vote.

When the Nation Was New

Our nation needed a plan for how the government would run. A group of leaders wrote that plan. It became the U.S. **Constitution**. The rules of the Constitution told how the president and members of Congress were to be elected. Yet, there were no rules for who was allowed to vote. The Constitution let each state decide who could vote.

The Constitution is not perfect. It does not include all the rules we need. The writers of the Constitution solved this problem by allowing for changes called amendments. Over time, amendments have changed the voting rules.

This woman is signing up so she can vote. Many years ago women were not allowed to vote.

At first, the only Americans who could vote were white men who owned land. Married white women were not allowed to own land, and most African Americans were **slaves**. Neither group of people could vote.

Soon after the Constitution was written, leaders added a part to the Constitution called the Bill of Rights. The Bill of Rights has ten amendments. These amendments were added to guarantee, or promise, certain rights. Yet, the Bill of Rights did not say who had the right to vote.

The Constitution was finished in 1787, but it was not until 1870 that the 15th Amendment became part of the Constitution. It said that states could not deny men from voting because of their **race**. African American men could then vote, but women still could not vote. When the 19th Amendment was added in 1920, women at last got the right to vote.

Even with these amendments to the Constitution, not all Americans could vote. People in towns across the country did not want women or African Americans to decide on government leaders. They were afraid of change. Groups in many areas did not want power given to the new voters.

A husband might keep his wife at home so she would be afraid to vote. Some states kept poor people away by making every voter pay on Election Day. Some states also added reading tests for voters. Many African Americans who could not read at the time were scared away.

The 15th and 19th Amendments were giant steps to guarantee Americans the right to vote. However, in the case of suffrage, which is another name for the right to vote, new laws were needed. Government officials passed laws that helped change things.

Eye on Votes

The Voting Rights Act of 1965 said that states could not stop voters from voting. After the law was passed, huge numbers of African Americans voted. In 1960 in the state of Alabama, there were only 66,000 African American voters. In 1966, there were 250,000 African American voters in Alabama.

African American Men Vote

After the **Civil War**, African Americans got many new freedoms. The 13th Amendment was added to the Constitution in 1865. It ended slavery in the United States. The 14th Amendment was added in 1868, and it said that all people born in the United States were citizens. This included African Americans.

Although many people worked to see that slaves became free, some did not think that former slaves should vote. Frederick Douglass was a former slave who made it clear that slavery was not over until African Americans had the right to vote. Frederick Douglass said that many former slaves were not really free. Officials still denied African Americans the chance to buy land or get fair pay for their work. Since the freed slaves could not vote, they could not change the way officials treated them. They could not choose the officials.

Congress agreed with Frederick Douglass. Leaders began to write and pass laws to help African Americans in the South. Congress said the states in the South that had left the United States during the Civil War could not be a part of the nation again unless all African American men had the right to vote.

Frederick Douglass believed that African Americans should have the right to vote.

Some African American men who were able to vote helped Ulysses S. Grant become president. Ulysses S. Grant worked with Congress on the 15th Amendment. The amendment said that no state or the **federal government** could stop a citizen from voting because of race or because he had been a slave. The 15th Amendment was added to the Constitution in 1870 while Ulysses S. Grant was president.

Just the Beginning

The 15th Amendment was a first step to guarantee that all African American men were able to take part in government. However, the states still had power to say who could and could not vote. At first, many African American men voted in elections. Many of them ran for local, state, and national office and were elected.

However, by the early 1890s, fewer and fewer African American men voted. People scared African American voters away in some places. They beat them and hurt them. Cruel people also tried to stop those who helped African American men sign up to vote. People were killed.

Another means to stop voters by race was to set rules at voting places. For example, some states made people show they could read in order to vote. At the time, many African Americans as well as many white people could not read.

Some states made their reading tests hard. A person may have had to read part of the Constitution. Then the person had to say or write what it meant. If an African American could pass the test, state officials might still say he could not vote. However, a white person who failed the test would often be allowed to vote.

Over the years, many African American men gave up on voting. When women gained the right to vote in 1920, most African American women were too afraid to even sign up to vote. Others who were brave enough to become voters were turned away at voting places. They did not try again.

African American men stand in line to vote in 1871.

The Voting Rights Act

In 1964 three people who signed up voters were killed. To remember them, hundreds of people marched in Alabama. Sadly, cruel officers beat people in the crowd. Many Americans were angry and wanted the government to take action.

President Lyndon Johnson had helped African Americans gain many rights. Now he wanted them to be able to vote without fear. He pushed Congress to pass the Voting Rights Act. "It is wrong—deadly wrong—to deny any of your fellow Americans the right to vote in this country," Lyndon Johnson said. "There is no **issue** of states' rights or national rights. There is only the struggle for human rights."

Congress passed the Voting Rights Act on August 5, 1965. President Lyndon Johnson signed the act into law the next day. The many ways people had been denied the right to vote were now against the law in the whole country. States could no longer give reading tests or make people pay to vote. The government sent people to sign up voters in states where there had been trouble. By the end of 1965, there were 250,000 new African American voters.

In 1965, hundreds of people marched in Alabama. They wanted the Voting Rights Act to be passed.

Eye on Votes

Many women worked hard to help African American men win the right to vote. Yet, at the time, women were allowed to vote in only one place—Wyoming.

Women Must Wait

The 15th Amendment made many women angry. They were glad that African American men could vote, but they had hoped that suffrage for women would be in the amendment. At the time, many people said that women were weaker than men and should stay home to care for their children. Married women could not own land. Many people said women should not vote. Women leaders knew they had work to do. Their struggle would take 50 more years before an amendment was added for women's suffrage.

Women Join Together

Women began working toward having the freedom to vote long before the Civil War. In 1848 the first big meeting for women's rights was held in a town in New York State. These people who strongly believed that women should be able to vote called themselves **suffragists**. Among the suffragists were Susan B. Anthony and former slave Sojourner Truth.

The women continued to meet every year. Sojourner Truth, Susan B. Anthony, and other leaders made voting the focus of their talks. Susan B. Anthony traveled the country to talk about what women could do to get the right to vote.

Woman suffragists from New York drive through their state speaking out for women's right to vote.

Sojourner Truth (left) and Susan B. Anthony (right) strongly believed that women should have the right to vote. Suffragists marched in a parade in Washington, D.C. in 1913.

Sojourner Truth spoke at a meeting for women's rights in 1851. She talked about her own life and told the crowd that she had always worked as hard as men. She felt that she should be able to vote. The women cheered! Sojourner Truth's famous speech was called "Ain't I a Woman?" The power behind this question stayed with the women who heard it.

Working for the Vote

The suffragists were brave and firm in their struggle to vote. Yet, they were divided. Some women pushed for voting laws in one state after another. Others wanted to fight for their beliefs in **court**. Still, many suffragists thought that an amendment was the answer.

In 1878 suffragists sent an amendment for women's voting rights to Congress for a vote. It failed, so the suffragists again worked for suffrage in one state at a time. In 1890 Wyoming became the first state to let women vote. By 1912 eight states in the west had joined Wyoming.

Some suffragists felt that the struggle was taking too long. They could not believe how hard it was to get the right to vote. Suffragist leaders began to reach out to the people.

Parades and Marches

The suffragists needed more people to join their struggle. They went anywhere people would listen to their views. They spoke in parks, at fairs, and on street corners. Then suffragists started to march in parades. They waved American flags. They carried signs that said, "How long must women wait?" Crowds came to the parades. Some people called the suffragists cruel names. Others cheered for the women.

A suffragist carries a flag as she marches in a parade in New York City.

When Woodrow Wilson won the 1916 election to be president for the second time, the suffragists thought he would fight for their amendment. When Woodrow Wilson did not fight for their amendment, they went to the White House. Women marched where Woodrow Wilson would see them.

Some of the women were put in jail for marching. Alice Paul had to go to jail for seven months. While she was in jail, Alice Paul decided to stop eating. By not eating, she got people to pay attention to her views. Alice Paul was set free after just five weeks.

Passed by One Vote

In 1919 Congress passed an amendment to allow women to vote. Then the states had to decide. At the time, 36 states needed to vote yes for the amendment to the Constitution, and 35 agreed. Leaders in Tennessee were divided. A man named Harry Burn was the last one in Tennessee to decide. He voted yes. With his vote in 1920, the 19th Amendment was added to the Constitution.

Eye on Votes

Many people in Tennessee were surprised when Harry Burn voted yes. They did not know that the 24-year-old man had a letter from his mother asking him to vote for suffrage.

The Future for Voting

The right to vote in the United States did not come quickly for women and African American men. After the 15th and 19th Amendments were added, other groups worked for more federal rules about voting. An amendment was later added so that people as young as 18 years old could vote.

Laws have also been passed to make sure that the voting amendments are working. The Voting Rights Act of 1965 was changed in 1975 and in 1982 to make the law better. This law now helps make sure that all Americans can vote. It helps citizens who are blind, who cannot walk well, or who do not speak English well.

In 2006, President George W. Bush signed a form of the Voting Rights Act so that the law and its amendments will be in place for 25 more years. This means that the federal government must continue to watch over the voting rights of its people.

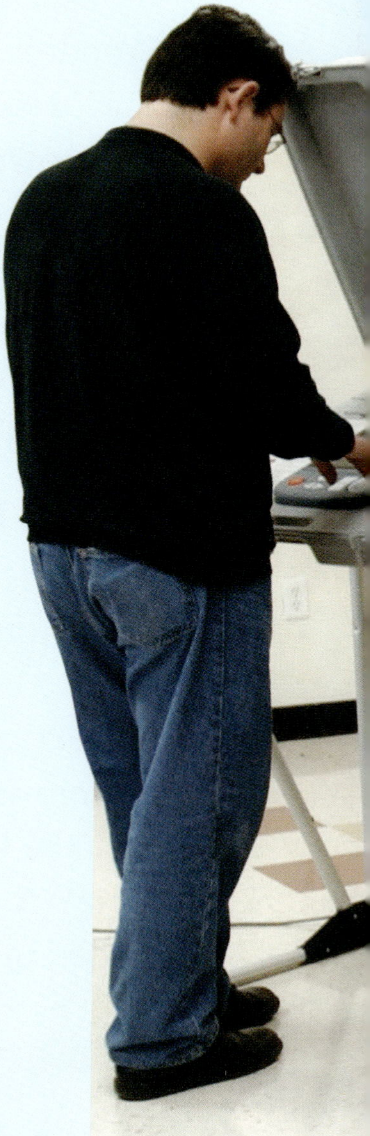

A man who cannot walk votes with other citizens.

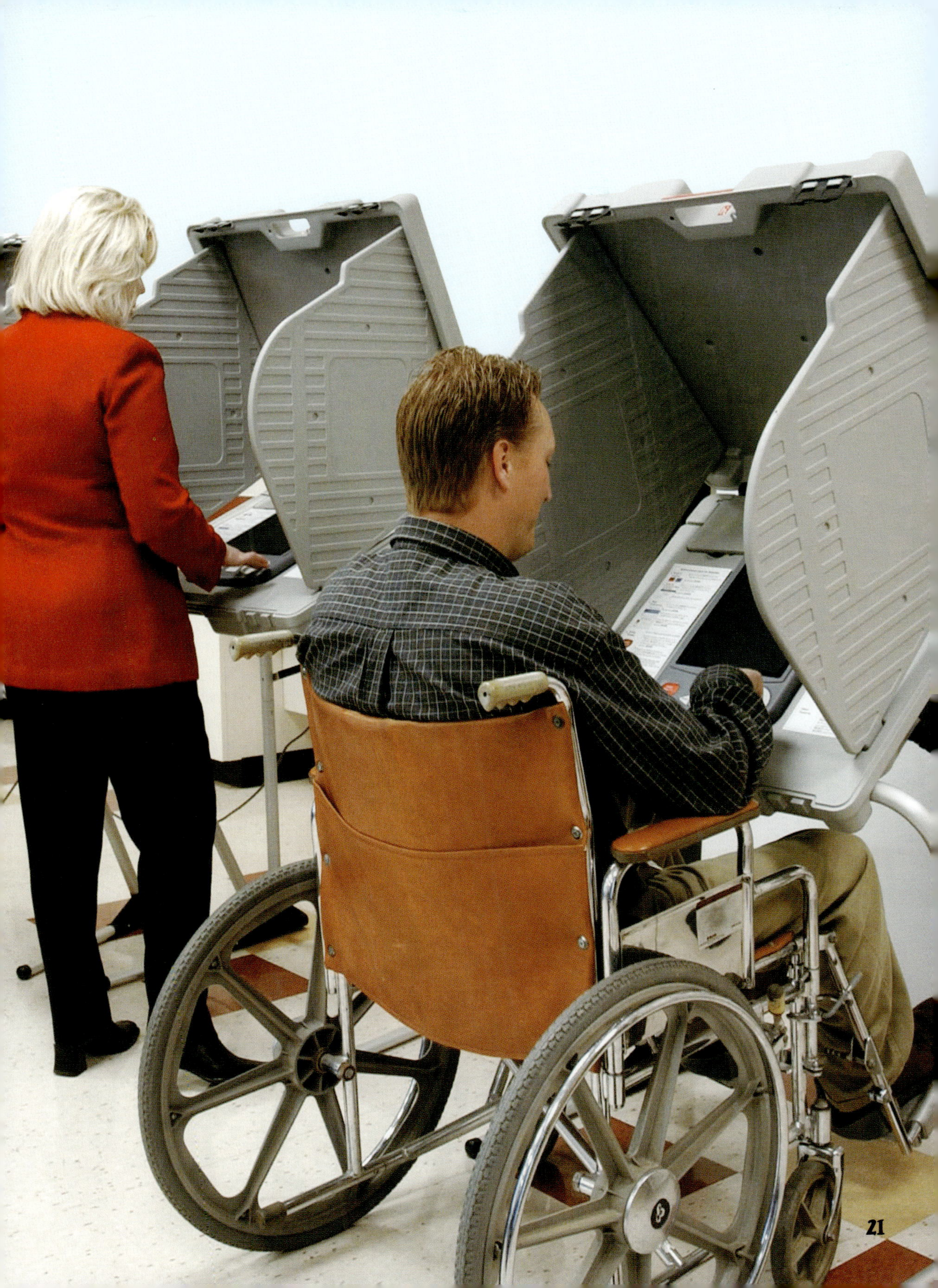

A Possible Amendment

Even with the voting rights changes, some people think that the Constitution and the courts can do more. The power to decide who can vote in the United States still lies with the states. Some states have passed laws that say people need to show a picture ID to vote. It may be hard for people who are old or poor to get this kind of ID. Federal courts may decide to let states choose these rules.

Important Voting Rights Events

- **1789** The United States Constitution takes effect and includes 10 amendments.
- **1848** The first big meeting for women's rights is held.
- **1870** The 15th Amendment says states cannot stop men from voting because of their race or because they had been slaves.
- **1920** The 19th Amendment gives women the right to vote.
- **1965** The Voting Rights Act of 1965 says states cannot stop voters from voting.
- **1971** The 26th Amendment changes the age when people can begin voting from 21 to 18.
- **2006** President George W. Bush signs a form of the Voting Rights Act.

The Voting Rights Amendment is new to Congress. The amendment, which was introduced in 2005, says that voting is a right of all U.S. citizens at least 18 years of age. Leaders who want the amendment feel that voting should be a federal right, not a state right. Others in Congress say the amendment is not needed. No one knows what will happen to this amendment.

Using the Right to Vote

Almost any American would say that voting is a great freedom. Yet, not all Americans vote. In fact, only about half the people who are allowed to vote actually vote today in the United States. If citizens do not like the way the federal government does its job, then they can share their views on Election Day. Voting is one of the best ways to make sure that the U.S. government represents the country's citizens.

Eye on Votes

Some national elections have been very close. In 2000, a different president would have been elected if only a small group of voters in six states had made a different choice.

Glossary

Civil War the war fought in the United States from 1861 to 1865 between the states in the North, which were against slavery, and the states in the South, which were for slavery

Constitution the paper that states the laws by which the U.S. government works

court a place where laws are carried out

federal government the central government of a nation that is a union of states

freedom a basic right that citizens have

issue a point to be talked about; a problem

race any group of people that share things such as skin and hair color

slaves people who are forced to work for other people for no pay

suffragists people who work for voting rights, especially for women

views the way people feel about something, such as the government